365 Days to Let Go

daily insights to change your life

Guy Finley

Inquiries should be addressed to:
White Cloud Press
PO Box 3400
Ashland, Oregon 97520
www.whitecloudpress.com

Cover and interior design:
Christy Collins, Confluence Book Services

Printed in Korea
First edition: 2007

Library of Congress Cataloging-in-Publication Data

Finley, Guy, 1949-
365 days to let go : daily insights to change your life / Guy Finley.
p. cm.
ISBN 978-0-9745245-5-9 (pbk.)
1. Devotional calendars. I. Title. II. Title: Three hundred sixty-five days to let go.
BV4811.F55 2007
158.1'28--dc22
2007022439

Table of Contents

Introduction

Solving the Mystery
of Letting Go

Sometimes the greatest truths are laid right before our eyes, in the simplest of things, and yet we just can't see them. Take for instance our own hands: what a miracle they are. If we consider for even a moment all they are capable of doing, we realize that a great wisdom sits hidden behind their incomparable design. But, with this thought in mind, permit me to add one more idea to help us see another part of their special purpose that lies "hidden" in plain sight.

What good would our hands be to us or, for that matter, to the world they are made to help shape, if all they could do was close down around something and cling to it? How stale and old everything would soon be for us if the act of "holding on" to things were all our hands had the power to do? Just imagine what life would be like if we were unable to touch anything new. Here's the point: to be able to touch and appreciate what is new, our hands are also created to open up and, as needed, to let go of whatever is no longer useful.

This same basic truth applies, even more so, when it comes to our need to release those old feelings and worn out thoughts that first clog up, and then compromise, our hearts and minds. These tiresome states of ourselves have become "stuck" within us because we haven't learned how to release them. But we can, and we will!

Once we understand that letting go is the missing half of the whole happiness our heart longs for—that it is a necessary and full partner in the power to discover and complete our True Self—everything about our life grows easier.

Old regrets dry up and blow away. We awaken to a quiet faith that fears nothing. New possibilities for us appear almost moment to moment because we've hung an "open for business" sign on the door of our life. And, as our contentment grows with who we are—*within ourselves*—we stop compromising ourselves and trying to win the approval of the world around us.

Best of all, as a result of our growing discoveries about the secret of letting go, we find ourselves on the threshold of solving the greatest mysteries: Who are we? Why are we here? And what is our true role in this world? For, as we start to see reality—as *it* is—in its timeless expression of creating life, perfecting it, and then letting it go, only to start all over again, we realize that we ourselves are an integral part of this Great Endless Story. And if the whole of life is being made new in each and every moment—and we ourselves are a part of its never-ending process of perfection—then letting go isn't some distant and difficult faculty to be acquired. On the contrary, letting go is an effortless state of our own consciousness; it is a natural power of ours needing only to be actualized in order for us to realize the freedom that it alone can grant.

Welcome into your mind the following images and insights. Taken together they help illustrate and illuminate a grand design in which we first see the wholeness of life—and then, as our awareness grows about this unfolding story, we enter into its native freedom. We are about to discover that more than being just a part of life's plan, letting go solves the mystery of it. We are about to see how the act of letting go completes the cycle of life itself. Now let's witness the truth of this beautiful idea in action.

Imagine: cold, stormy skies break open, and the dark clouds shed their coat of winter snow or let loose their soaking rains.

Soon after come the bright days of spring; the earth lets go its frosty grip on countless seeds buried within her—giving birth to new grasses, flowers, and trees.

Time passes, bringing warm summer days and nights; sweet fruits fall from the trees that can no longer hold onto them.

Now, carried along by gusting fall winds, helpless leaves rush in no direction until released by a stillness as sudden as their flight. There they rest until driven on again into the shelter of some unknown refuge.

Each of the four seasons, their countless stages, all the actors appearing there: clouds, rain, earth, grasses, sunlight, trees, fruit, seeds, winds, and dancing leaves—all serve to reveal a great, silent, and unseen story called "Letting Go." This story is a mysterious one, for it is played out upon a stage that is itself contained within a greater stage hidden just behind it—much in the same way as a single sound stage operates within the larger motion picture studio that oversees its shooting schedule. And, to help complete the picture, this studio complex is, itself, but one part of a still larger entertainment corporation. The point here is as follows: each of these stages upon which we see life unfolding holds another stage and is, in turn, held by a still greater stage, infinitely.

The only thing that changes (and everything does!) on these stages of life—from sub-atomic levels all the way up to and through the expansive cosmos itself—is the size of and character of the actors moving upon and through them, the endless cast of creatures playing out the act of letting go. Again, let's see!

As summer trees must cast off their ripened fruits, so the whole summer season must submit itself to the coming cooler days of fall. And, accordingly, as the earth turns, each season must let go and allow the coming season its time and place—even as the earth itself must yield to the sun's influence over the whole of her body. But neither has the sun any choice when it comes to releasing the fruit of its abundant radiant energy. For in letting go the sun not only provides life-giving forces for all created to receive them, but also lights up all the stages upon which life has been made possible because of it. As little, but wise Yoda of *Star Wars* fame would say: Grand, it is!

Now we have come to the most important question of all: where is our place in this extraordinary life? What is our role in a reality that unfolds as it does because the continual act of letting go makes all things possible? Let's take a moment to see what is right before our eyes.

Do we not each go through what we can call the personal "seasons of life" during our lifetime on earth? We have all known, according to our years and experiences, the sweet springtime of youth, the deep summer of fulfillment, the bittersweet fall of letting others do for us what we can no longer do, and the chill

9

Introduction

of winter. Coming to the close of one's life is itself but a passing season in an unseen greater one. Do try to see the timeless beauty in all of this change, and you will.

Is any one of us less than a rose, or less than the single raindrop that—in falling to feed and refresh the flowers—makes it possible for them to open and reveal their rainbow of colors and fragrance for us? The answer should be evident.

We are more than the rose, greater than the solar radiance that stirs her essence to bloom. For neither rose nor sun's radiance is conscious of the great story they serve as they let go and give themselves up to life.

In truth, we human beings are created unique among all things that take life and then give it back on the stage of life, *for we are made to witness this eternal story* . . . and more.

We are not made to have only a relative role in this Great story, to be—as are all other creatures—just a minor, passing actor upon its stage. No, the promise of our potential far outweighs even our ability to imagine it, for *we have been created to consciously participate in its timeless telling*.

When Abraham Lincoln, the great American president, looked at his country so torn apart by the conflict of racial hatred—born of individuals clinging to ways of life that sorely compromised the soul's longing for an inclusive love—he said of this world of troubles: "This too shall pass."

Of what world was he referring to in that moment? Did he speak of a nation at war within and upon itself, that *it* would pass? Or did he address the state of his weary heart, so heavy with despair over the condition of man, so filled with doubt as to the course he must choose to help change the consciousness of the United States?

Clearly he was referring to all of these conditions, and more. He was saying that these trials, along with their attending troubles, *will pass*. But how could he know this truth when darkness had spread itself out both before and within him at once?

Lincoln knew, as can we in our battles with unwanted moments, that the events he faced—as awesome as they were—represented only a single page in a far larger story. His eyes could see the truth behind what the world remains blind to: this unending and ever-unfolding life in which we dwell *requires the passage* of all the pages that have gone before it.

Letting go, at its heart, is an act of agreement with Life; it is an accord on our part with the mystery of the present moment, unfolding as it does to reveal us the truth of ourselves. And each new revelation brings with it a silent request, brought to our attention by what has been stirred up within us. In these telling moments Life is asking each of us: "Will you be a witness to my story? Will you let go of your short-lived moment in the sun of passing circumstances – in order to realize that just behind all such shadows dwells my Life whose Light never fades? Will you choose in favor of entering into a Life whose story never ends, and in which fear and failure simply do not exist?"

What must we choose so that we can participate in this Greater Story?

We must choose to let go.

Winter

If fall signals the retreat of nature—as when the last leaves fall from the trees and countless creatures crawl into nooks and crannies to pass through the bone-chilling days to come—then the first day of winter, December 21, is when nature—having gradually withdrawn her forces—reaches a resting point. Now comes a three-month period of time that represents a pause in the activity of life.

Great lakes, ponds, and streams freeze over; the earth grows hard and unreceptive. Tree sap stops flowing. Even the air becomes dense, slow to move, and heat stealing. Yet, not everything is as it appears to be!

The pervasive stillness and deep silence of winter are powers every bit as great as are the explosive forces of spring and summer, only different. After all, what is a glacier but a vast frozen river crawling its way through time? Both are forms of water whose unstoppable might can carve their way through solid rock! So, how can we channel this power of winter and use it to let go of whatever stands between us and the higher life we desire?

Winter is the time of the year when the forces of nature assume their most passive form. But we are discovering here that passive does not mean powerless! Consider the micro-pause between each beat of the heart. Is the heart less alive, made less potent for the brief rest it takes in its own beating? Of course not! In each such moment of its repose we could just as easily say that it is gathering itself for its next pulsation. In other words, its temporary passive state is actually a measured act of preparation. So it is with the "heart" of winter.

The better we understand this unique power of being passive—and how it serves as the secret consort of all things active—the more we grow in the faith we need to be wisely passive toward whatever fears remain in us about letting go of our false self. This is why, during the dark days of winter, we should take time each day—as often as possible—to quietly return to the living Light that dwells in the center of ourselves.

By gathering our attention in this way, and bringing the whole of ourselves into the heart of this interior stillness, we not only collect our own forces, as nature herself is doing, but much more: in this deliberate act of gathering ourselves—and for the conscious sense of quiet contentment we find within it—we are also being released from the false idea that the source of our strength and security can be found somewhere outside us.

The great French author, philosopher, and Nobel Prize winner, Albert Camus, knew the power of this truth now revealed.

He also realized its liberating potential. In the following carefully chosen words, see how beautifully he tells us not to fear any season of life wherein we find ourselves feeling empty, alone, or without any Light in our life. He writes: "In the depth of winter, I finally learned that within me lay an invincible summer."

Once we start to see, to know in our innermost heart, that life itself is already complete, we can let go of whatever—or who-ever—would have us believe otherwise.

Old attachments and their long-standing aches are now seen for being what they have always been: appendages of days gone by, worthless to the Higher Self we have agreed to become and by whose stillness we realize this need for a wholly new valua-tion of our own soul.

Now is the season to die to discontent, to withdraw our con-sent to live with any thoughts or feelings that would convince us it's necessary to live in conflict or confusion.

The winter season can be the most challenging in terms of learning to channel its powers to help us let go. But, we may also have this timeless assurance: we are really created to enter into the perfect stillness from which we came. And for our return home—by entering into the bare infinity that is the center of our True Self—we arrive where we have always longed to be …

without ever having had to set out. Here we make this last, glad discovery: the task of letting go, of separating ourselves from who and what we need no longer be, has already been done for us.

January 1

If we will only work to remember that we live in a world within which there are an infinite number of stories unfolding—all at the same time—then we will never forget that it is our choice as to which of these stories becomes our life.

January 2

We are created with the tools it takes to master our own lives. But self-mastery remains the ultimate mystery until that day dawns when—weary of struggling to overcome what we blame for our conflicted selves—we let go and enter into the untamed country of ourselves by becoming completely still. And by this stillness, we tame its wildness; and through this stillness we are given dominion over all the kingdoms of heaven and earth.

January 3

The source to which we turn, and from which we derive our strength, is the real mark of our character; for in any moment of trial, no one can be any stronger —better or brighter—than what he or she loves.

January 4

Uncertainty is unwanted because it feels so unpleasant each time it appears in our lives. But can we be awake enough to see its positively bright side? For as surely as darkness must come before the break of a new day, so it's true: before the new light of higher understanding can have its gentle dawn in us—we must see that we have come to the end of what we know.

January 5

Every time you reach the conclusion that you cannot go past a fear, doubt, or other perceived limitation, you deny the source of your own endlessness!

January 6

When at last you decide that you would rather find your own way through whatever stands in your way, you will also find, at last, that you have found yourself.

January 7

The real test of our love for the light of truth is not when life is bright, but is best measured when nothing goes right. For the love of light at mid-day is easy; but to remember it in the dark of night—to struggle to recollect ourselves into its sheltering glow—demands a conscious choice. Are we to be the one who feels forsaken by the light we profess to love? Or will we be the one who never forgets that true love never dies?

January 8

We affirm the light of Truth—not by professing its powers on sunny days, but in choosing to walk by its light—no matter how faint—even in the midst of our darkest hour when all that we see before us is defeat.

January 9

Your True Self cannot be made a captive of any dark condition any more than a sunbeam can be caught in a bottle.

January 10

Things go wrong in life. They just do. And sometimes downturns feel like they'll never get back to right-side up. Life is like that. So what! What we have been given is not what makes us who we are; the true measure of our soul's success is what we make with what we are given.

January 11

The past is as powerless to darken the present moment as is a shadow to reach up and drag down the form that cast it.

January 12

When we know that life, bare as it may be at times, is the most precious gift of all, then ours is a peace beyond profit and immune to loss.

January 13

Since what troubles us, troubles us now—then *now* is when we must awaken to and address *within ourselves* whatever it is that makes us ache. To delay this interior work is to lose sight of the doorway that our own disturbed state opens for us and beckons us to enter.

January 14

The more time we spend considering the shortcomings of others, the smaller a person we become.

January 15

In our conversations with others, we must learn to say what we want as clearly and kindly as possible, but leave no doubt as to our desire.

Otherwise we learn, too late, the painful lesson that unspoken assumptions always return to bite the hand of those who hold them.

January 16

Some of God's greatest gifts to us often appear, at first, as though He is taking something away from us.

January 17

Thinking can no more produce peace of mind than throwing a stone into the center of a pond has the power to end its ripples.

January 18

Better to see where we have been blind in this life—toward others and about ourselves—than never to see at all; otherwise, we'll just go on blaming whatever walls we walk into for getting in our way!

January 19

The only thing we "add" to life by our resistance to it is the weight of a self-induced suffering born of needless worry.

January 20

Dreaming of some brighter day to come—
when, for happier circumstances, you will
be freer—is like believing that the solution
to living in a city with unending traffic is
to have a better car to sit in as you go nowhere.

January 21

Sitting in judgment of others, and reaching the conclusion that their lives are meaningless, does not prove that our life has meaning.

January 22

Not only is beauty in the eye of the beholder, but so also is ugliness—a simple truth that those who fear self-knowledge fail to see. The wise understand that truth is always beautiful, even when it is hard to look at.

January 23

If we would examine closely the strands of those unseen webs that seem to catch and hold us captive every day, we would see that they are nothing more than the stuff of our own thoughts—spun off by a mind never quite content to be where it is with what it has.

January 24

Nothing glows brighter than the heart awakened to the unseen light of love that lives within it.

January 25

Allowing any fear to assure us that being frightened is a necessary first step towards winning a fearless life is like believing that if we run fast enough through a rain storm we won't get wet!

January 26

Whoever fails to try what his heart would have him do—because his mind tells him, "This you cannot do"—fails to hear the ever-present Voice of Reality forever shouting to all those who would dare: "No sincere effort ever goes without being rewarded."

January 27

Here is one of the great spiritual mysteries of all time. Freedom is either found within one's suffering or not at all; the only thing one escapes when running from pain is the possibility of discovering its purpose and how to transcend it.

January 28

There are times when the greatest acts of kindness we can express toward another human being is to swallow our own sadness, or to refuse to make that sarcastic or impatient remark. Act of kindness such as these cost us ourselves, and when we agree to pay this price, we buy back a better, brighter world.

January 29

Much as ocean tides surge and ebb upon waiting shores—always changing, yet changing nothing—waves of thoughts or feelings that pass through our bodies cannot hinder our True Selves.

January 30

One thing that makes negative states so difficult to drop is the illusion they create within us that no choice exists for us other than to cave in to their punishing presence. But, in truth, it is not we who are without choice in such moments: it is the negative state that has no choice but to disappear once we remember that *no* darkness is greater than the Light.

January 31

What causes our suffering in life is not in what life itself brings to us, but the way in which we identify with self-limiting negative states as they convince us that it's only wise to refuse what we have been given.

February 1

What you fear might happen to you *is* happening to you while you fear what you do!

February 2

We do not see life as it is, but as we are; and so when it seems to us as though our life is not enough, not right, or just not happy, it isn't because life has singled us out to deny us its fulfillment, but because we have cut ourselves off from its abundance by being all tied up in "nots"!

February 3

We spend so much of our time caught up thinking about how to succeed with our personal escape plans that it never has a chance to dawn on us that our True Natures cannot be made captives of anything!

February 4

We cannot hope to change the unwanted world that we experience without first working to change those parts of us that are, at present, creating the world that we feel needs to be changed.

February 5

What is hard on us is not life itself, but the hardened way in which we tend to think towards it; so that it is nothing other than our own thoughts that turn naturally passing moments into unyielding tablets of stone from which we then read and weep.

February 6

The real reason why nothing is ever gained by running away from our troubles is that the only thing really troubling us is our own fearful, but mistaken, belief that we need to run away from anything.

February 7

The potential power of any healing idea is only as great as we are willing to submit ourselves to the light of its truth.

February 8

See the ocean: it does not run after its own waves, as it knows they must return to rest in its depths. And so it is for us: whether we speak of joy, peace, strength, or love itself—no greater illusion exists than that we should somehow find, searching outside of ourselves, the source of our True Self.

February 9

Those who cling to their pride deny them-selves, by their own preference, the action of a love upon them that alone is empow-ered to release them from their pain.

February 10

Trying to make yourself feel better by imagining a happier time to come is like hoping to make the pain of being hungry go away by reading a menu.

February 11

Only a mind awakened to itself knows the cost of being spiritually asleep, while the mind slumbering in itself knows nothing—not even the cost it pays for remaining asleep.

February 12

Life is always new, which means there is no such thing as an "old" problem. What does, in fact, grow "older" in us—and secretly seasons our suffering—is how we more readily and rapidly accept our own conclusions that our problems are insurmountable. And so, as amazing as it is, we remain captives of our unwanted condition by consent!

February 13

We are never captives of anything other than the illusion that the negative condition that holds our attention for the moment is the only reality available for us to know.

February 14

Nothing in the universe has the power to hold the human mind in painful captivity except for the cage the mind builds for itself out of its own mistaken thinking.

February 15

Real wisdom begins with growing weary of seeing how your best answers for how to live always leave you with a heartache.

February 16

Seeing yourself as being "nothing" in the world does not make you something; nor can this resistance protect you in any meaningful way. On the contrary, the only one who comes to know the lasting contentment of true spiritual fulfillment is that unique person who realizes the fear of emptiness is itself an empty power.

February 17

Once we understand how to use them, life's many unwanted twists and turns are no longer seen as being just isolated, disjointed experiences under whose yoke we are born to be burdened; they are realized instead as unique opportunities whose rewards are the lessons needed for the education of our souls.

February 18

The true measure of one's strength is not determined by drive, assertiveness, or even willingness to suffer for the sake of some worldly desire. Instead it is found in the degree to which one will agree to enter into the struggle between the indwelling light and darkness.

February 19

Until we learn what it means to come to
a complete inward stop, nothing of a true
spiritual nature can start within us.

February 20

Nothing in the universe has the power to stop you from starting your life all over, nothing except for one thing: unconsciously identifying with those punishing parts of yourself that want you to believe that wherever you may have been stopped along the way is the same as having gone as far as it's possible for you to go.

February 21

For those with ears to hear—whose hearts
are set upon discovering Truth: some things
cannot be learned about the nature of light
while the sun is shining.

February 22

Once the mind has been touched by something it can't imagine—a deft quieting embrace—it gladly gives up its childish pursuits and waits in receptive repose.

February 23

We are only as capable of receiving true higher guidance as we are willing to turn loose the tiller of thought, raise our eyes from the horizon of self, and wait quietly for a star not yet risen to reveal the way.

February 24

The unwanted condition itself does not make us stuck; we are hung up when re-living thoughts and feelings about our situation. To be new, we must learn to see ourselves from that part of us that knows who we really are; our True Nature is not created to be a captive of anything!

February 25

True self-remembrance begins with be-coming conscious of what happens to us in our forgetfulness. The truth can only set free those who remember how much they are in need of its rescuing light.

February 26

Just as it is impossible for a ship to drop anchor and then leave port while still being chained to the bottom of the sea, so is it impossible for us to cling to our regrets in life and be able to move on from there at the same time.

Just as a frightening shadow cannot pass away until the form does that casts its scary appearance, neither can we hope to go beyond our own dark inner states until we voluntarily transcend the level of self that gives rise to them.

February 28

Learning how to love deeply, and yet to cling lightly to what we love, is a razor's edge. The more identified we are with what we would hold closely to our breast, the more we must cry when life runs through its inevitable course. All the losses we suffer either further teach us this lesson of lessons, or we deny its truth, and in so doing, condemn ourselves to suffer the necessary consequences.

March 1

The true measure of our life is not determined by the kind of events we are given to
meet, but rather by what kind of person *we
are* when we meet them.

March 2

In any relationship, the one who is hurt most by the absence of compassion is the one in whom compassion is absent.

Painful negative assumptions about our-selves that darken our hopes for a higher, happier life are much like thorns on the stem of a fragrant rose: the only power they have to hurt us is when we mistakenly close our hand around them.

March 4

Honest self-examination is always the best prescription for whatever troubles the heart. The light of higher self-knowledge not only reveals those secret places within us where our pain hides, but its enlightening action upon those still darkened places begins their healing transformation as well.

March 5

The sooner we remember that there is no power on earth that can hold our True Nature captive, the sooner we are released from that prison of negative thoughts and feelings that we so often mistake for being the same as ourselves.

March 6

We are never farther apart from what we love
than our ability to remember its presence.

Real peace is not an agreement between others; it is a personal act of sacrificing the self that believes others are responsible for the reality it experiences.

March 8

Our present experience of life, its happiness or sorrow, is nothing more or less than what certain unconscious parts of us tell us it is. Before we can hope to change our life experience, we must stop trying to rewrite the Book of Life and work instead to awaken ourselves from the dreams of the unseen storyteller within us.

March 9

Allowing your mind to reach *any* unhappy conclusion about the limitless possibilities of your life—and then agreeing with it because you now see yourself through the narrow eyes of that negative state—is no different than believing the tip of your nose is the end of the world!

March 10

Whenever unhappiness lingers on—so much so that we start believing darkness has won the day—we may find new strength to start life over in this bright truth: the only cause for our continuing sense of feeling so bound and restricted is that we have agreed—without knowing it—to live in a world smaller than our potential. We must let go of whatever may be limiting us.

March 11

Being fully present is the best guarantee for
a bright future.

March 12

Freeing ourselves from feeling helpless in the face of conditions that seem beyond our control is as simple as awakening ourselves in that moment to remember this self-liberating fact: a deep illusion has no more reality to it than does a shallow one!

March 13

Whatever happens in life happens as it must in that moment. So our efforts should not be with struggling to control the way things unfold, but rather in working to awaken from our own sleeping nature that punishes us each time it is not allowed to live out the dream that it has divined!

March 14

Anger, fear, resentment, and blame are not the bitter leftovers of whatever you think blew into your life and battered you around. Negative states are a storm *in themselves*; to see them as such is the first step towards anchoring the vessel of your soul in a safe harbor.

The strength of any weakness living within
us is the degree to which it is feared.

March 16

We must do the work to prove our fears groundless; otherwise, our fears will gain ground, and our lives will be spent in their service.

March 17

To see that the places where we feel stuck in life are really secret passageways—provided for us to gain vital insight into our own greater potential—is to no longer perceive these hurdles as a hindrance to success in life. In fact, once we learn to welcome whatever challenges us, we stand at the threshold of a new order of our own being, where never again will we feel ourselves to be a victim of anything!

March 18

The secret purpose of that self-loathing nature in us—that wants us to suffer today for what we could not do yesterday—is not there to help us make straight our mistakes, but rather to ensure that we waste the rest of our days struggling to escape the ache of useless regrets. Awake! Detect and reject despair! It is not the guiding light it seems to be, but it is a cold heat that compromises any heart into which it seeps.

March 19

No one fails who falls in the battle to be a better human being, for while the flesh is often weak, Spirit is indomitable—and always rises anew, strengthened for its experience and ready to start again.

March 20

Isn't it strange that whenever wisdom is needed, we seek the words of those who have been through the greatest trials; but when some painful trial visits us—to bring us the wisdom it alone can provide—we want no words with it!

Even though we all have our natural preferences, no season of the year is greater than any other. Each plays an indispensable role in a cycle of life and each one serves the season that follows on its heels, enabling it to fulfill its purpose in a procession as timeless as the earth itself.

The first day of spring marks that moment in the turning of our world when a "great dawning" begins that takes several months to culminate. To understand this idea, we need to see how all of life is in "scale."

For example, just as the sun rises each morning to dismiss the twelve hours of darkness that came before, so the appearance of spring signals a similar moment—only in a greater scale of time; for with the dawn of the spring, the many dark months of winter must loose their collective grip, giving way to a gently increased measure of light and warmth that stirs the earth from its slumber. During this time of the year, it would be easier to stop the earth from spinning than to stop the surge of new life being awakened within her.

Seeds buried in the earth are broken open from the inside out, made to release their delicate shoots of grasses, herbs, and flowers that reach for the light above them. And, as if by magic, along the sides of seemingly lifeless branches appear silver-green buds of baby leaves that stretch out to unfold themselves like banners in the sun.

Life is beginning again everywhere, and so can we, *if* we are willing.

The power of spring lends us the fresh forces we need to break through and to let go of old patterns. During this time of the year, the possibility of making a brand new beginning in life is never greater. Why is this true? Because spring also dawns within us, and if we will align ourselves with the power of its presence, then the unstoppable principle of rebirth itself will work for us.

How can we harness this planetary power for our own good? Here are just a few of the many ways we can work with spring to start a new life for ourselves:

All past wishes lying dormant within us—to outgrow old limitations—should be brought out into the light of our longing to transform them and be left there to bathe in our need to be free. Whatever conditions in life may have once overcome us should be re-challenged now, regardless of past results.

And, as spring marks the return of a celestial light that gradually grows greater than the darkness it has come to dismiss, so is this the best time to stand up and start walking through whatever frightens us.

Spring

We should work to detect and detach ourselves from old heartaches, keeping our eye on emerging possibilities, instead of looking back at lost opportunities. By acting in this way—as though we are free—we find that what once held us captive no longer has the power to keep us down. We succeed because we have become partners with the light of Real Life.

Lastly, spring is a time of great and natural tension for all living creatures on earth. Nature sows into every last one of her children an urgency to seek out their "other" and to procreate in order to ensure the continuity of their species.

Each spring great forces are released to work upon and within us. Life is literally seeking itself through us, asking us to open ourselves and receive what will renew us. But, if we would receive this new life, with all its promise, then we must be willing to sacrifice within us whatever stands in its way. We can only be made as new as we are willing to let go of who we have been, and springtime not only awakens this need within us, but it also grants us the possibility of its realization.

What is that first, faint intuition of something greater than ourselves, other than the Herald of the Heart quietly announcing the existence of a whole new level of being above us—and asking us, at the same time, if we will prepare ourselves to receive it?

March 22

If we are to know the truth of ourselves,
then we must test ourselves, for in no other
way can we discover that boundaries belong
only to those bodies to which they apply;
and that our minds, at last unfettered by
fear and from other false apparitions, may
know freedoms as unattainable to the flesh
as is the open sky to the starfish that dwell
at the bottom of the sea.

March 23

The things we think ourselves to be cause our heartache and pain, for there is no such sorrow in the still whole depths of who we really are.

March 24

The first step in dismantling any dark negative state is to remember that it has no right to occupy either heart or mind.

In each moment of life we must choose to take the upward path, or we lose the opportunity to rise above the parts of ourselves that like to fall down.

March 26

Wishing for freedom is like wishing on a star: until we learn what it means to personally reach out and help produce that brighter world we envision for ourselves and others, we remain little more than armchair architects—those who believe that merely dreaming of a world without fear and hatred is the same as building one.

March 27

The best time—in fact, the only time—to make a real change in your life is in the moment of seeing the need for it. He or she who hesitates always gets lost in the hundred reasons why tomorrow is a better day to get started.

March 28

We cannot change what life brings to our door until we learn to change the way in which we answer it!

Our reluctance to throw ourselves into life with all that we are—to abandon ourselves, come what may—is born of the fear we may not *be* enough to succeed. But the truth is within us dwells more than we take ourselves to be, and only by leaping do we learn of unseen wings that open only in midair.

March 30

We make first contact with the unshakable character of our True Self when we stand on the unknown ground of an unwanted moment and see there is no need to fear or to fall into despair.

March 31

Throw yourself into what the day asks of you, and let no thoughts of uncertainty delay your departure. For the only true way to answer the day is to sail into it, despite contrary winds, and let whatever unfolds teach you to master the ship of yourself.

April 1

We all long to be known. The unspoken hope of the heart is that something greater than ourselves already knows the undiscovered places in our souls, and only waits to show us all that we are. But, as yet, we don't know ourselves—and true self-knowledge is the secret partner of this longing that accepts no other lover.

April 2

Once we realize that whatever we bring into our awareness has always existed in our own consciousness, only not yet awakened, we also understand this liberating truth: *nothing exists outside of us*. All destinations are already within us, including the love we are searching for and the unconditional freedom that it alone has the power to grant.

April 3

The true test of our actual level of understanding is how we respond to those moments in life when we don't understand why life unfolds as it does.

April 4

A great spiritual paradox: the knowledge
we gain of any weakness that lives within us strengthens self-understanding. To
know this truth is to welcome those shocks
in life by whose light we become more and
more wise.

April 5

Believing that getting anxious or agitated over a problem helps to produce a positive outcome is like yelling at a campfire on a cold night to hurry up and burn hotter!

April 6

Failure is never to be feared; we must never bow before what seems to lay us low. Better our attention should be turned to our false ideas about the nature of success—and to see there, beneath its gilded veil, the face of the cruel master whose slave we have agreed to become!

April 7

Here is a great spiritual truth: the only time we ever fail at anything in our lives is when we walk away from a challenge before we've allowed it to teach us its lessons.

April 8

Intuition is a glimpse of a world just above you; attention is a toehold there, but our working intention to remain awake in these higher realms is our passport to possibility and the promise of what we might yet be.

April 9

No one succeeds in realizing real freedom who—when life seems to conspire against this wish—is turned round by this trouble and starts defending the reasons why he or she must live as a captive for yet another day.

April 10

Every inspired thought—each new insight that points to the heights of what we might yet become—serves to enlarge the mind that conceives it. And the grand discovery of that mind touched by any such truth is that within this breaking light is found nothing less than the endlessness of its own possibilities.

April 11

Billions of people miss this obvious fact: to go anywhere in this world of ours requires that we start out right from where we are. So it holds equally true that only by working with what we are in the moment can we ever hope to reach and realize the heights within ourselves.

April 12

To do those works required of us, to act from what we know is right and true—*even when we don't want to*—is the first step of giving birth to something in ourselves that gradually gives us, effortlessly, everything that we need to be right and true.

April 13

Patience is an important but unseen part of letting go—not unlike learning to tolerate the small thorns that grow on the stem of a rosebud. But why would we agree to suffer in this way? Because we know that when, at last, the new bud blossoms, its gentle fragrance proves our passing pain to have been worthwhile.

April 14

Whoever loves to sound his own horn, soon finds himself playing all alone!

April 15

Whenever we collide with any event and then run away from the scene of the crash, we lose the opportunity to discover that the only collisions we have in life are with what we have yet to understand about ourselves.

April 16

Real Success in life is not determined by measuring up to some preset social standard of accomplishment, but is found through the individual effort it takes to go beyond what blocks our way in the moment. Such a deliberate effort in the face of our own doubts and fears always proves these negative states powerless, which is the same as discovering we are *already* free.

127

April 17

No one on this earth can be what *you* already are; so stop trying to imitate what you were never intended to be, and start awakening to all that life itself has made possible for you to become.

What is the essence of true character if not the realization that, in the moment of challenge, the pain of yesterday's blow is the seed of tomorrow's strength?

April 19

Real faith and true freedom go hand in hand, because no one is free who lives with fear, and fear cannot live in the one who has faith.

April 20

We can only begin to change the world around us when we are willing to become a conscious part of *all* that is changing.

April 21

We are not here on earth to change our destiny, but to fulfill it.

April 22

The answer as to what is the best use of one's life is found in being present enough with oneself to detect and reject all of those useless thoughts and feelings that undermine our higher possibilities. Only then do we realize that letting go of these limitations is the same as serving our own highest interests, for our greatest potential is to be free!

April 23

The reason it's necessary to swim upstream at times is because on the other side of the resistance is the flow.

April 24

The exploration of a new territory must pre-
cede the possibility of claiming the natural
treasures uncovered there; this same principle
holds true when it comes to the undiscovered
country of our own consciousness: we must
be willing to explore those still secret regions
of our present nature if we ever hope to realize the extent of its limitless resources.

April 25

We must learn to reach, moment to moment, for what seems above and beyond us if we are ever to be touched by the light of our own True Self.

No weakness of ours persists that is not fueled by the unconscious fear we have of it; so to wake up and face this fear is the first step in erasing the weakness that it protects.

April 27

We need never accept the presence of anything in us that wants us to ache over who we are—or are not—for it is given to us to outgrow ourselves anytime that we awaken enough to see the need for it. And when is there a better time to let go of who we have been than when it is trying to pull us down?

Just as the petals of a rose need sunlight and fresh air to release their fragrance, so do people who wish to awaken to real life require the light of Truth and what it reveals within them in order to blossom into true human beings.

April 29

Seated in the center of the heart, as surely as the essence of a tiny seed holds the
promise of a towering tree, dwells in us the
presence and power of a greatness whose
living light can dispel any gathering darkness and change unkindness into conscious
compassion.

April 30

We must choose whether to live our lives in the endless struggle of trying to fit ourselves into life as this world has given it to us—or to work to give ourselves that Life that all else is created to fit into.

May 1

Real freedom isn't subject to how others estimate our value; it is found when we realize that none are free who measure their sense of worth against another's standard.

Though we find no evidence of anything noble in someone who has betrayed us, neither is there anything noble in our bitterness.

May 3

The true path to greatness is found in our willingness to walk toward, and then through, whatever may be seen in that moment as being greater than ourselves.

May 4

If we will persist with our wish to be true to ourselves—to be kind and patient, caring and wise in the face of any setback—we realize this all-empowering truth about ourselves: in this life we each have but one weakness and one strength. Our weakness lies in what we have yet to discover about ourselves; but our strength is the realization that in each of us lives a Columbus of the soul. There is nothing in the universe that can remain hidden from the one who will dare to discover the truth of himself.

May 5

There is no such thing as "later" when it comes to our spiritual life. What we do in the now is the sole seed of our life experience.

May 6

Seek first freedom from fear, and find there, in this interior liberty, the lasting fulfillment only Truth can give. Then, in this new richness, you will be able to do in life what it is you really want to do and, without doubt, be successful because you have first succeeded as a human being.

May 7

The reason we should hope for the success of others—even if we temporarily fail—is because time proves that whatever perfection one can achieve . . . becomes the possibility of all.

May 8

When we realize that there is no place on earth that can be any better or different from what we are when we get there, then we will no longer believe in some new destination as a solution for an old suffering. Instead, we will do the interior work it takes *to be* what and who we are, for at last we have understood that the only safe haven is our own awakened state.

May 9

Never believe in any negative thought or feeling that would have you believe, "There's no way!" Always remember instead that real life is a secret and vital flux of possibilities rising up from the ground of what seems improbable, much as a spring flower manages to bloom in a once frozen field.

May 10

The light of awareness first reveals to us hidden, stagnant aspects of our own nature, and then acts to liberate us from this mistaken identity, leading us to further integrated and higher states of consciousness.

May 11

No one ever walked the path of greatness who was not first visited by Love, who whispered the way.

May 12

Real achievement—the true measure of how we have advanced in life—is not determined by what we have acquired, but rather by the degree to which we have put our fears behind us.

May 13

If we could only remember in those un-wanted moments—when we see where we have been wrong in life—that this vision is granted us because we have just been vis-ited by some new light by which to see and know ourselves more truly, then one day we might come to welcome what now seems so unwanted. What does it take to welcome every moment of one's life? Love the light!

May 14

The seed of greatness is sown in an instant, but in this world of ours, everything great takes time to grow. Patience, mingled with persistence, is the special nutriment that sustains all things great. Therefore, should we wish to win the great life, we need only add equal measures of quiet watchfulness to our spiritual willingness and a great goodness cannot help but flourish within us.

May 15

From daisies in a field to suns ablaze in distant galaxies, everything is always flowering. To sense this truth is an act of grace; to know it's true, is divine.

May 16

Wisdom always recognizes herself. Truth knows the sound of itself. Love never fails to see where love is not. The living Light within us sees by its own luminescence, and never dims or goes out.

May 17

Contrary to popular belief, God did not create us to look upon His life as a wish-fulfillment center. Instead we are created to live in the awareness that God's life is the center of our being, and that to realize this relationship answers all of our wishes because Love itself has then become our life.

May 18

Learning to be grateful for the lessons hard learned is the secret and greater lesson hidden within all moments of the soul's education.

May 19

We should never measure ourselves according to our "possibilities" because all such estimations of self are always based in secretly embraced evaluations of our own past; rather, we ought to give ourselves over to what seems impossible to us because we are only truly fulfilled in this life to the extent that we are able to transcend who we have been!

May 20

Just as winter yields to the onset of spring, as surely does the moon submit to the sun, so too are we created to give ourselves to that Greater Life that alone can make us ever-green and fill us with life-giving Light.

May 21

The wish to escape a trouble is trouble's wish, which explains why so many of our troubles are born with a wish!

May 22

The mastery of anything, including ourselves, begins with the faith that we are not
here on earth to be perfected according to
an image we hold of ourselves, but rather,
to allow perfection to work its way upon us,
so that only the awareness of something
greater than ourselves can draw us into a
greatness beyond ourselves, if we will it so.

May 23

No one fails who will try, try again; everyone fails who won't begin!

May 24

Just as the sun rises to fill a darkened morning with its soft new light, so does the living
light of Truth descend into the willing soul,
transforming its earthen elements and res-
urrecting them into a spiritual temple ablaze
with God's eternal light.

May 25

Spiritually speaking, the cost of starting over is not what we pay to achieve some distant desire, but is in our willingness to let go of— to dare to live without—any desire we may have whose promise of fulfillment drives us to search for it in yet another tomorrow.

One cannot have a true wish for the love of God without it being God's love making that wish (within him or her)—any more than one could wait in hopeful anticipation of a sunrise who had never before stood in the warming rays of dawn's early light.

May 27

Only what awakens us to our own immortality truly profits us. All else serves only to gently rock us into a fitful sleep in the stream of passing time.

Fear is what happens to us whenever we forget that the One who created us fears nothing. True courage is remembering this truth and then daring to act upon it in the face of a fear. There is no other cause of fear, and no other true solution. Awareness of this truth awakens in us the action that sets us free.

May 29

If we must dream, let us long for that life beyond ourselves; for who desires things already known, or otherwise imagined in forms reconfigured from fantasies too well worn? Behold: the unknown life calls to us from a desire untold; too distant and dark to be seen, but nearer to us than the very light in which we dwell.

May 30

The fear we feel that we can't succeed with starting life all over again is because our old nature wants us to believe that the path to our new and True Self requires we retrace our steps and fight our way back to an unsoiled starting place in life. But here's the truth: there is no pathway, past or future, that leads to real self-newness. The secret place of all fresh starts in life unfolds right from where we are in each moment that we dare to leave who we have been behind us. Start now!

May 31

We must learn to see that our true dwelling place is not that mind filled with the incessant chattering of our thoughts, any more than the ceaseless chirping of branch-hopping birds is the same as the deep and quiet forest in which they dwell.

June 1

Be encouraged by this truth and then do the inner work to realize the freedom it holds for you: life itself never stands in our way. It never intends to hold us down. If something is seen by us as restricting our way, then, instead of backing away in resentment from what amounts to a vision of life provided for us by our own thickened thoughts about what we cannot be, let us turn our attention to the parts of us that habitually believe in such barriers and learn to walk through these false notions as we do through late afternoon shadows.

June 2

When we understand that our true purpose in life is to grow in the wisdom of God's plan, and that this wisdom we seek itself seeks us to help its goodness be revealed, then we also realize that whatever disappointments we encounter along the way must themselves be a part of wisdom's eternal plan.

Into each of our lives comes some fight that must be made; however, the key to true self-victory is not that we win at all costs, but rather that we remain true, kind, and innocent in spite of the costs.

June 4

As we wake up to those parts of us that would have us believe we can change our lives by following the directions of the very self that we no longer wish to be, then we are on our way to winning a new life. The real spiritual journey begins with letting go of who we have been instead of calling upon it to be our travel guide.

June 5

Learn never to blame another for the pain you feel, nor to complain about anything that life brings to your door; but this doesn't mean to be accepting of those who would see you ache, nor should you be apathetic in the face of anything that challenges your hopes and aspirations.

June 6

Our earthen hearts must hold within them some bit of heavenly soil, for what other explanation is there for how quickly they fill and swell into gladness whenever the love of God rains down and soaks into their dried-out grounds?

If people could tell the difference, and were allowed to speak only original impressions, the world would suddenly fall into a deep and sweet silence.

June 8

Much as the waters of a river run through a valley, helping to turn native fertile earth into tillable soils capable of high productivity, so do invisible streams of spiritual currents course through the soul, intended to transform dark potential into the light of purpose fulfilled.

Let us work to lose our fears themselves and not become the poor captives of what they would have us believe must be protected; for what good is it to stand guard outside the front door of any house into which thieves have already broken?

June 10

The day of our spiritual awakening is the same as the delightful date of our departure from a bankrupt world filled with beggars dressed as kings and queens.

June 11

The more we lose our patience, the easier it becomes for us to give it away.

June 12

It isn't until the ground drops out from beneath us for the hundredth time that we suddenly realize falling down is not our only option. Faintly, but surely, if we will listen, another law in our own nature calls us to realize its power: we can catch, suspend, and drop our own weighted reactions. And so it goes that we slowly learn to take wing.

June 13

When we learn how to be still, to listen to what life would teach us, we discover that not only is there a plan already in place—a celestial curriculum designed to instruct us in the ways of its timeless peace and power—but that the universe itself is a school for our higher education.

June 14

Any weakness we may harbor in our present character persists only because we have yet to see how its presence compromises our happiness; but a growing awareness of this interior shakiness changes everything. Our awakening stirs within us a celestial character created for the purpose of transforming the soul's stumbling stones into the building blocks of a whole new unshakable self.

June 15

Letting our plans for life take the place of actually living is like hoping to catch the delicate scent of a rose by flipping through a book on how to successfully grow a flower garden.

June 16

Learn to rely upon yourself in all things, and you will make this glad discovery: the strength you find yourself lacking is the seed of the new strength that you need to succeed.

June 17

Anyone can chart a course to happiness, as millions of people do on a daily basis; but only the few who refuse to fall into despair after losing their way ever find what they are looking for.

June 18

To merely long for the higher life is not enough; it takes spiritual perspiration to turn our aspiration for celestial heights into a permanent station.

Properly understood, everything in life that now disturbs us is intended to lead us to a world in which who we are lives as one with all that takes place within it.

June 20

Just as an acorn that goes unplanted in the earth can never realize its destiny to become a mighty oak, so it holds with any real spiritual principle that we unearth in our journey through this life: only those truths developed in us—by reason of our work to see that they take root in the ground of our soul—are empowered to grant us the strength, shelter, and sustenance of their eternal life.

Summer

One of the secret reasons why summer is a welcome time of the year is because as temperatures start to gradually rise, so do our spirits! After all, who doesn't feel better after a day by cooling waters, a late-afternoon walk, or spending a balmy night on a deck with family and friends? But, there's more to summer than its simple pleasures. As we're about to discover, this season is full of secret powers that, once understood, are guaranteed to help us let go and grow!

On the summer solstice—June 21 [in the Northern hemisphere]—the earth is bathed in the greatest amount of sunlight possible and with all this radiant energy comes a period of peak activity experienced everywhere in nature.

In the trees, life-supporting sap flows more freely than at any other time of the year. Leaves burgeon and swell; countless individual branches reach for the sun, even as root systems dive deeper into the earth. Creatures everywhere are searching for—and consuming—the vital foods they need to nourish the explosion of growth taking place within them.

Summer fruits start transforming the substance of their own flesh into sweet sugars, dressing themselves in rich colors that proclaim they are ripe and ready to eat. Fields of grains and grasses reach maturity; their stalks, waving in the late-afternoon winds, are teased into dropping countless seeds.

Summer is the time of natural abundance. These are the days of a great conversion: the whole of life flourishes, fulfills, and feeds itself at once. We see before us the immeasurable power of *plentitude*. But what do we stand to gain for realizing the strength of this season?

When we know that nothing can be added to something to make it greater than it is—when the present moment of life is as full as life permits—then we should also be able to see the following truth: anything that appears within us—that would try and tempt us into searching for our contentment in some brighter tomorrow to come—*must itself live outside the fullness of the now*. And whatever lives outside the true power that beats the heart of the present moment is powerless to do anything—let alone deliver us into a state of being whole. In the bright light of summer, we are empowered to detect and drop the only thing that ever defeats us: being identified with the false self that wants us to feel discontent with what life gives to us.

With these last few thoughts in mind, summer is a good time for letting go of any fearful concern we may have over uncertain days that lie ahead of us. Any part of our false self that wants to feel troubled over its own darkly imagined tomorrow should be tossed high into the air—winnowed like summer wheat so the chaff of fear blows away—leaving behind only the precious kernel of contentment with what we are being given in the here and now.

This season of growth is also the perfect time to detect and dismiss any parts of us that tell us we can't outgrow what may have compromised us in days past. It is the time to discover that this higher ground we seek more than just awaits us; it is actually reaching out to meet us half way, if we will only take the necessary steps in our journey of letting go.

Summer is also a secret time of sacrifice; it marks nature's perpetual passage from one form into another. Again, the evidence is everywhere: flowers shed their petals to reveal the baby fruits hidden in their buds, even as other maturing fruits ripen to reach maximum sweetness, only to fall to the ground as food for those who find these seasonal gifts.

Letting go takes place naturally as we grow to see that whatever we will release of ourselves is returned to us, only transformed into something greater than what we thought we gave away.

Whenever we will actively surrender ourselves to God, to the Life Divine, then we aren't just relieved of nagging worries, fears, and doubts; these lower estates of consciousness are replaced with higher ones. For our sacrifice we are given a whole new self that lives in a world of light where dark states cannot dwell.

June 21

If our sole wish as we walk through this life is to draw nearer to the heart of God, then with each step taken in that remembrance, we arrive.

June 22

To be able to grow in heart and mind—which is the true benchmark of a successful human being—we must learn what it means to give all that we have to whatever it is that we may be doing in the moment: for only *complete* action on our part has the power to teach us completely.

June 23

Work to connect yourself to the "allness" of life, instead of to the smallness of it, and you'll awaken to a new kind of greatness already living within you.

June 24

If, each day, you will use the strength you have been given to do what life asks of you, not only will you grow stronger every day, but you will also witness an increasing willingness to embrace those tasks in life once thought too great to bear.

June 25

Once we understand there is no flower, no leaf, no limb, or branch that is greater than any other part that grows on the tree of life, then we realize it is more than enough to be just what we are in the moment.

June 26

It is what we are willing to learn in the un-folding moment, and not what we think we already know, that finally turns the tide of any trial in our favor. This is why the wise ones have always taught that knowledge is the seed of wisdom, but its flowering is in conscious action.

June 27

Do what is in your power. Refuse to do what is not. It is not in your power to change the nature of what has past, but you can let go of those parts of yourself that want you to cling to some pain past in order to keep it present!

June 28

It is said that "beauty is in the eye of the beholder," but this truth tells only half the story. Whenever we see something of beauty—and take into ourselves that loveliness—we ourselves are transformed into something now made beautiful. And so it is with any state of being to which we give our attention!

June 29

The one strength that never turns into its unhappy opposite is the true self-understanding that who *you* really are is not, and never has been, whatever weakness is seen within.

205 *Summer*

June 30

The more we practice quietly stepping outside that rushing stream of thoughts about
ourselves, the more we realize our True Self
as being something altogether unthinkable;
for the undreamed power of a silent mind
is this: Since it never sinks itself into useless
considerations of the painful kind, it has no
need to be rescued from its own troubled
creations!

July 1

Whatever we consent to embrace in life—
including unwanted events that may cause
us to suffer—adds to our lives a measure of
love.

July 2

Unless heart, head, and hand are all in the same place at the same time, working as one, whatever is done is done half-heartedly, without thoughtfulness, and in half-measures. The only way that heart, head, and hand can be all together at once is when love unites them in a single purpose.

July 3

The reason perfect love casts out fear is because any unwanted condition willingly embraced loses its power over us. We are never captive to what we agree to, nor do we wish for a time to come when we will be free. Only when we are no longer driven to imagine a freedom apart from what the moment holds for us, will we find that we are free now.

July 4

The real quality of life is not determined by
what we have won from it, but by what we
have discovered within it.

When it comes to true success in this life—
regardless of whatever world it is in which
we strive for excellence—there is no greater
ability than to be able to do what we don't
want to do, when we don't want to do it,
and, in all cases, to do it well.

July 6

True freedom is found in neither position nor possession: real liberation is the moment of release that takes place whenever some inherent limitation is acted upon by something greater than itself and transformed accordingly.

July 7

You have triumphed at life's game when—no matter win or lose in the eyes of the world—you can walk away from any demanding moment with a measure of more true self-understanding than you took into it.

July 8

Patience can be a great virtue, while learning to push ahead often proves invaluable to those who prevail; but only a marriage of these two spirits can grant us true success, because in their union we are empowered with a calm and steady watchfulness that is always ready and willing to act.

July 9

When we see the truth that the more we struggle to get ahead in life, the further it seems we must go to get there, then we will know why the wise ones teach that nothing is more profitable for us to do than attend to the present moment, and to work there to possess ourselves within it.

July 10

The longer we continue to make excuses for ourselves, the shorter grows the time between the events that compel us to do so!

The more we keep the company of truth, and work to remember the good of it (even when we are feeling bad), the more our lives will share in the presence of a goodness that not only protects us from our enemies, but serves to perfect us during every encounter with them.

July 12

In order to enter into the school of the eternal, we must allow the lesson in each moment to be our teacher.

July 13

Practicing the presence of God doesn't necessarily change what comes to us, only *who* it is that it comes to.

July 14

To be persistent is to work for the cause, even when it has gone underground and goes unseen for a while. Then, for our efforts to rise above ourselves—though they may feel pointless when all seems well— we ascend to a new and unshakable interior ground that doesn't give way when our conditions change once again.

July 15

Before we can see God's Life in all things,
all things must be for us, God's life.

July 16

There is nothing higher, better, or brighter for us to do with our lives than to use every moment for the purpose of attending to what truth would have us learn about ourselves.

July 17

The quiet awareness of true stillness tells an untold story of a whole that is greater than the sum of its parts.

July 18

The true individual is one who doesn't need the approval of others in order to know the peace of mind one finds in being just oneself.

July 19

What lies ahead of you, its joy or sorrow, is already within you.

July 20

Our doubts are traitors dressed as protectors, but all they actually keep safe is the fear they harbor that we might outgrow them and their limiting hold upon us.

July 21

The present moment is the canvas of creation: our perception, a palette of primary colors; our actions, brush strokes—while thought provides both background and texture. To know these things is the beginning of the artful life.

227 *Summer*

July 22

No moment can be any more valuable to us than our awareness of the possibilities unfolding within it, which means that real success in life doesn't so much depend upon what life hands us to work with, but rather into whose hands we place whatever has come our way.

July 23

The best we can do for others, to help make their lives brighter, begins with the work of enlightening ourselves. In this manner—from our first tentative steps toward a life in the Light, all the way to the summit of higher self-understanding—we agree to the task of never again allowing ourselves to darken the world of another.

July 24

At any given moment, we must give all that we have to whatever we may be doing, for only complete action on our part has the power to teach us completely those lessons that life would have us learn.

July 25

One reason the wind of good fortune is often found at the back of people who are
successful in life is because these individuals are usually found moving ahead of it. . .
in anticipation of its arrival.

231 Summer

July 26

What is the real gold of any moment save the higher wisdom gained from it? The treasures of this world come and go—the playthings of conditions beyond our control—but those truths we glean about ourselves, and the goodness born of their light, belong to us forever.

The human heart is both wine cellar and crystal glass; to drink deeply from its private reserve requires only that one enter into it with a silent wish to taste the divine.

July 28

There is only one way to make every moment count: we must be awake to—and present within—each new moment if we are to ensure ourselves of its proper accounting.

The task of completing ourselves in this life only really begins with the discovery that our lives are a part of a far greater story than we can tell ourselves; and it isn't until we find ourselves in this larger Life that our own life reveals its secret true proportion.

July 30

We think that what troubles us most in life revolves around those things we can't control, or that we're otherwise unable to possess. But, the real source of what torments us is this: we don't possess ourselves.

July 31

Before we can know a happiness beyond the reach of conflict or sorrow, we must ourselves be whole; for any happiness apart from self-wholeness is only half a happiness and must, in time, prove itself so.

237 *Summer*

August 1

All tempests in nature must pass just as psychological storms must pass too; but those who run from their troubles run with them, which is why—wherever they go—a storm awaits their arrival.

August 2

Understood aright, every circumstance in life—no exception—is created as a part of our continuing preparation to know God's perfection.

August 3

Whatever it is that you wish to receive from life, learn first to give this without reserve; but neither should you give in order to receive, for this is a secret form of taking that brings you nothing in return but resentment.

We cannot be considered the true captain of our own vessel in life until we realize that while it is our duty to be on deck at all times with our eyes on the horizon, it is the wind that moves us and the sea that keeps us afloat.

August 5

Real fearlessness comes with knowing that
we have everything we need to succeed in
the same moment that it's needed.

August 6

The only one who never loses sight of his true nature, who never becomes a captive of negative states, is that fortunate person who never forgets this one great truth: even though nothing we look upon in this world belongs to us, everything about our life is a gift.

August 7

In direct proportion to the strength of our remembrance of His life does God grant us His strength.

August 8

Look at what a person labors at and you will know what he loves. Look at what a man loves and you will know whom he serves. Look at what a man serves and you will know his master. Look at a man's master and you will know his destiny.

August 9

The great and telling power of patience, coupled with persistence, is that whoever will pay for their company throughout this journey called life cannot help but succeed at reaching their heart's desire.

August 10

No one who drinks from the Cup of Truth shall perish; for truth is the Light, and the Light is forever—having no beginning or end.

August 11

Patience is a great virtue acquired, in part, by awakening to what our impatience does to ourselves, as well as others.

August 12

No one finds freedom who believes that their liberty depends on some consensus of how others view either their choices or character.

August 13

The unexpected pleasure and power of a quiet mind is that such stillness effortlessly holds—and realizes as its very own—everything that moves within it without itself being moved.

August 14

The secret fragrance of the present moment is the understanding that real life is forever flowering.

August 15

Beauty is more than just the experience of a unity greater than thought can measure; beauty gives evidence—through our awareness of its expression—that no observer exists apart from what is observed.

August 16

Each moment of life is only as precious as is our ability to attend to it.

August 17

The unexpected sweetness of any perfectly silent moment is that we enter into it through a still secret part of ourselves that is its perfect reflection.

August 18

One simple guideline for finding yourself in any crowd of stressed or confused thoughts is to remember, right in their midst, that *you* are none of them.

August 19

It only *seems* that there is something more important for you to do than to just quietly be yourself.

August 20

What doesn't go right for the one who understands that, once awakened to real life, nothing can go wrong?

August 21

In this life, because of its invisible laws of perfect reciprocity, anything that we do to help another outgrow the limitations of his or her present nature produces the same order of growth within ourselves.

August 22

Life is going according to God's plan only
if you are.

Summer

August 23

Learn to act in the moment—do as this moment asks—and life won't have to give you a kick to remind you of what you are supposed to do!

August 24

When we realize that our true nature can never be known, only continually discovered, then we become the fearless explorers of reality we are created to be—moving in and out of complementary or conflicting moments alike with the same ease as does a dolphin take delight in carving its way through the endless currents of the sea.

August 25

Getting angry and resenting someone who doesn't treat you with the respect you expect is like using a sledgehammer to swat a fly that has dared to land on your forehead!

August 26

Just as the still waters of a quiet pond effortlessly mirror the depths of the sky that tow-
ers above it, so does the silent mind reflect
with ease the Divine that dwells within it.

August 27

We do not cease to exist when, having surrendered ourselves to the starlit depth of a dark night sky, all thought subsides; or when, for the invisible touch of an unsought love, our heart is filled with a gentle stillness; rather only within moments such as these—when we are enabled to forget about ourselves—do we really live!

August 28

To live, to really live, means to take one's part in real life; and real life is always testing herself, which means *to really be alive is to be tested*. But real life never asks more of herself than she has to give, so it isn't until we accept, willingly, whatever trials life gives us that we are truly given real life.

August 29

One good reason to work at simplifying one's life is that fearlessness is the natural fruit of innocence.

August 30

Spending our time in quiet contemplation of truth, or simply practicing being still so as to discern the Divine within ourselves, is the same as finding answers to problems *before they appear!*

August 31

In this life, due to the great and compassionate intelligence that governs it, not one thing is wasted … and this includes, once we come to realize our own foolishness, even those moments of our lives we have unknowingly thrown away.

September 1

We may say that we have found our true place in life—a place undiminished by time, unassailable by tide—when we know that this place resides in the very center of our heart and we seek it nowhere else.

September 2

The main reason to hold our chin up whenever some negative thought tries to drag us down is that whichever of these two directions we choose first in that moment is what the rest of us will follow.

September 3

The terrible twins called worry and anx-
iousness can be taken up, reduced, and returned to their basic nothingness by that
mind brought back into its native quietude.
Learning to be still is not just the remedy
for our self-wrecking states, but also proves
to be their permanent cure.

September 4

What makes someone a master is not that he or she possesses some unattainable skill, but that these individuals have first realized the existence of, and then made contact with, a world above them that wants to pour its more perfected understanding into their own.

September 5

True silence is, in part, the pleasurable sensation born of a quiet time taken in nature, as it is the natural repose that comes quietly at the close of day. But, in truth, silence is not a feeling at all; it is to one's emotions as is the sky to the sunlight that streams through it, lending it life.

September 6

Whatever is true, right, and real in any human being need no more seek approval for its own nature than does an eagle in full flight hope to hear the "caw-caw" of some crow below it, calling out to it about how confident it looks soaring alone through the wide open sky!

September 7

Enlightenment is not knowledge of the whole universe, but to be conscious of, and act in accordance with its perfect design and divine purpose.

September 8

The secret inlet into the realm of what is timeless and eternally true is our awareness of the present moment; for our awareness of now is not an awareness of a given time, but is vested in that higher consciousness through which the things of time move in and out of creation.

September 9

Things always change in life, but for those who put the life of truth before all else, these changes lead them to what is changeless.

September 10

Whenever we will put ourselves on the side of what we know is true, then Truth takes our side, lending us what is noble, needful, and divine. Truth sees to it that we are strengthened by wisdom, sheltered by light, and that our hearts know the peace of having fulfilled God's plan.

September 11

Weak thoughts and feelings often feel strong, but remember, real strength is never anxious, cruel, or punishing.

September 12

Real wealth is not measured by how much we manage to take from life, but is realized in discovering our endless potential to give something of ourselves to each moment, enriching everything in it, including us.

September 13

Just as we can't toss a pebble into a pond without making small waves that spread out to touch its banks, so is it true that our sincere spiritual effort makes ripples in unseen realities, waves that touch and transform the shores of the soul.

September 14

When, before our inner eyes, we always have someplace better to be, or that feeling we must make something more of ourselves, we miss seeing two great truths: first, all imagined destinations are dreams whose promised fulfillment fades the nearer we draw to them; and secondly, where and who we are *in each moment* is a field of possibilities whose riches are not only immediate, but everlasting.

September 15

Whatever you have conquered within yourself is forever conquered wherever and in whomever you have occasion to meet it again.

September 16

The best definition of integrity is searching only your own conscience for confirmation of what is good and true, for that which is good and true is not social in nature, but spiritual in need and in deed.

September 17

The only way we begin to act as a true force
of healing in the lives of others is when, at
last, we cease to hurt ourselves.

September 18

Show me that rare individual who grows weary of giving his or her life away to win some fleeting sense of fulfillment born of an equally temporary thrill or pleasure, and I will show you someone being prepared for a relationship with a love that never dies.

September 19

If we went through our day tending half as much to the care of God's business as we give to our own affairs, then—from the resulting light of gladness seen spreading across the faces of family, friends, and strangers alike—the good truth would be obvious: taking care of God's business is what's best for our own!

September 20

Being at peace, and learning to live with quiet confidence—even as the world spins wildly around us—begins as we realize within us the presence and power of an interior stillness that neither needs, nor searches for, anything outside of itself in order to quietly know itself.

Fall

...and the Winter Solstice

Although it varies slightly from year to year, the start of the fall season is usually September 23, the autumnal equinox. This date is auspicious because it marks the onset of a great, but mostly unrecognized, cycle in life.

Just as we learned how the outward-bound powers of spring and summer unfold themselves in a show of creative splendor, so too the fall season never fails to reveal its unique character, only *in reverse!*

Autumn days signal a new kind of activity; it's the time of the year when nature makes her quiet retreat, a return journey back into the great "storehouse of life" wherein she will rest for a while before becoming active once again.

We see this same dynamic principle of outflow and inflow over and over again, operating on stages as small as quantum particles, all the way to the cosmic seasons of the sun itself. Think of it: we human beings breathe in and out, moment by moment receiving and then releasing vital air. Each day the ocean tides rise and fall, even as the moon moves through its monthly cycle of waxing and waning.

But here is the all-important key: these vital forces that oversee and enforce life's ceaseless expansion and contraction, that ensure fullness becomes emptiness in order to fill again—they have no conflict with one other. Far from it: they secretly serve to complete one another. This knowledge can be our power because—with such wisdom in hand—we can let go, knowing that whatever we release will be returned to us in a whole new form. It is law.

Fall is nature's preparation for regeneration, and we, too, should use this time to release those dreams of ours that have proven themselves to be fruitless. In fact, anything left hanging over—from the heartache of an unresolved relationship, to that argument with someone that still stings us each time we relive it—should be deliberately dropped now, shed like dried-out leaves to blow away in the winds of time.

The fall season, so full of autumn colors, tells the passage of one order of life surrendering itself so that another may take its place. This transformation makes it a natural time for us to let go of any old resentment—to forgive those who may have hurt us—so that our heart, willingly emptied of the pain of the past, has room within it for the arrival of a new order of joy and trust.

As we watch the life-force of nature withdraw itself during these last three months of the year, we see fields of green turn from gold to brown. Leaves lose their sheen and fall, without ceremony, to the earth that will consume them. Still, in all of these changes we know there is nothing to fear. Great nature must take its rest in order to resume being active again when conditions allow. It is our time as well to embrace this natural repose, letting go of whatever lives within us that wants to drive us forward without regard for our need to rest.

"To everything there is a season"—so goes this tried and true ancient wisdom. Fall is the season for gently stepping back from whatever it is that we endeavor to be in life; it is the time for honestly evaluating our own pressing desires in order to discern the difference between what genuinely serves us and what simply enslaves us.

Learning to let go in this way honors life, because it is true to what Life needs in order to succeed within us and through us.

September 21

To be able to see beauty, find comfort, and
feel secure in the midst of any change that
life may bring to you is the first fruit of
awakening to the changeless Self.

Fall / Winter Solstice

September 22

No brighter tomorrow can dawn for us that isn't paid for each day by our work to better serve God's life, illuminate our self, and uplift the hearts of others.

September 23

Always remember, regardless of what be-
falls you in the moment, to hold your head
up high, for who you really are is not made
for low places; you should not agree to
dwell there in the darkness.

September 24

Real love does not embrace what is unkind, cruel, and without conscience in human beings; yet it allows for it, knowing that all things dark and destructive must one day pay—by an act of love—for their thoughtless expression.

September 25

The difference between learning to consciously suffer a negative state versus unconsciously succumbing to its darkness is the difference between learning how to saddle a stubborn mule to carry you where you wish—or—having to carry that mule on your back wherever you go!

September 26

The longer we take any illusion to be real,
the less illusory do we believe it to be.

September 27

Instead of being the source of our daily sorrow, everything in life that passes ought to prove itself a part of our ongoing joy. For hidden in the deep of this ceaselessly changing river of life runs this healing discovery: whenever we stumble and suffer over some unwanted remains of the day, it is we who have stepped outside the flow of real life, and our pain is the price for wanting to be a world unto ourselves.

September 28

The true depth and breadth of the heart is measured not only by what it can hold, but also by how willing it is to let go.

September 29

We are only truly complete, in the real meaning of the word, when we are in communication with the world above us and conscious, for its presence in us, of a tender outflow of which we are the intended vessel.

September 30

Just as tumbling leaves in the wind make the wind visible, so does the need of someone—that stirs the heart of another to answer it—reveal the presence of a love greater than either person, yet that lives as one within both.

October 1

We must love God more than we long to have the experience of His love, for real Love does not fit into the mortal heart; it surrounds and envelops it as does the sweet apple its seed, keeping it safe and sustaining its presence until it can be released to glorify that greater life that gives it birth.

October 2

The truest form of art is to mold each moment around your understanding that nothing in the created universe has the right—or the power—to make you unhappy.

October 3

The fabric of the false self is made up from innumerable strands of experience woven together by an imaginary tailor who lives in terror that what it has made will unravel.

 October 4

In the same moment you can see there is nothing to talk to yourself about that is worthwhile listening to—you will feel the faint stirring of a sweet new silence within you that braces the soul with a strength unexpected.

October 5

Spiritual wisdom is our greatest wealth and,
as we realize the truth of this—so that true
self-knowledge becomes our single greatest
wish in life—each moment of every one of
our relationships serves as the secret path
to the summit of ourselves.

October 6

Only those who never give up, who persist with their wish to find and fulfill the promise of themselves, make this truly self-liberating discovery: places once seen as being impassible barriers to happiness become as bridges to the same, but only if they are welcomed as a part of the journey.

October 7

The unattended mind is the breeding ground
of self-defeat.

October 8

The price of possessing ourselves, of being empowered to live with a calm mind and a compassionate heart, begins with the conscious act of letting go of our "tomorrows" so that we may know ourselves in and through each and every moment of our day.

October 9

Not wanting events to unfold as they do often feels like a measure of control over unwanted moments, but any negative reaction to reality is only an unseen form of self-punishment and not the rescuing power we mistake it to be. The only thing our resistance to life adds to us is the weight of a self-induced suffering born of a needless worry.

Fall / Winter Solstice

October 10

The fear of stepping up to life, of coming right out and asking it for what we want, ensures that not only won't we win our heart's desire, but fairly well guarantees— for our obedience to negative doubt—that we will never realize the peace of a quiet mind that has seen how life itself wants to grant wishes that are true.

October 11

Either we learn what it means to lead by example, or we are lounge-chair leaders who have deceived ourselves into believing that our ability to criticize those who go before us is the same as having reached the top of the mountain before them.

October 12

If only we would see that the degree to which we ache over any given moment is the secret reflection of what we make of that moment, then this unseen making of our own aching would end!

October 13

Every daring dismissal of what we have already been is a conscious invitation to what we are yet to be.

October 14

Real power isn't the ability to imagine an endless series of solutions to old problems, but to awaken the higher understanding that allows us to transcend the need we have to live with any painful problem at all.

October 15

Some will tell you that it is wise to never forget the pain of the past. But if you look closely at the anger, sorrow, and bitterness that has hardened their faces, then you will also see why learning to forgive is the better of the two paths.

October 16

Worry and uncertainty cannot be solved by the mind that creates these self-wrecking states. Only by allowing such fears to run their full course through the mind that has made them can that same mind come to see how it makes its own misery. Then fears are not resolved—they are dissolved.

October 17

Here is why a mind awakened to its own native silence never gets into a stew over what to do with any negative thought that appears within it: just as light makes obvious whatever form is brought into it, so silence can see a troubled thought for what it is in reality—nothing more than an agitated noise fashioned into a familiar shape—a discovery that, once made, requires nothing of us other than to just let the pain of it fade away.

October 18

Whenever we can remember that we would rather smile about what life brings us than suffer over it—that our natural preference is happiness, not hurtfulness—then in such moments we are being mindful of what we love most. Similarly, can't we also strive to remember how much better it is, for everyone, to brighten the life of another rather than to darken it in our forgetfulness?

October 19

The reward of being true to ourselves becomes more and more apparent as we realize that most of the fears that stalk us are created by us when we are false to others, or to ourselves; too late we discover that to compromise our own integrity is the same as forsaking our wish to be fearless and free.

Fall / Winter Solstice

October 20

Until we learn the one great lesson that what *we* want from life must play a secondary role to what life asks of us—which is to grow in the timeless qualities of selflessness such as self-sacrifice, kindness, and love—then we will remain unable to share in the abiding sense of peace and freedom that comes to us only as we realize the true purpose of our being.

The imitation of greatness gives rise to fear, but when we dare to be ourselves—in spite of the fears we must face for our wish to be real—we awaken within us the character of that greatness we long to know.

October 22

If we ever hope to have right, bright, and truly kind relationships with others—where we never again lash out at anyone in order to feel better about ourselves—then we must awaken enough within ourselves to see that wanting to punish another for the pain that we feel is the pain we feel.

October 23

If we will only dare to give everything we are to whatever we may be doing at the moment, we will always find that when that relationship reaches its natural end we have been given more than we had at the start. It is law: to be filled anew, we must be willing to empty ourselves of ourselves time and time again.

October 24

Show me someone who isn't working to improve whatever it may be that he or she is doing—every time they do it—and I will show you a person who is missing the very purpose of being alive.

October 25

We too seldom stop to weigh the relationship between our own negative states and
the weary world around us that these dark
thoughts and feelings help create in our ab-
sentee ownership of them.

October 26

Every time we reach the conclusion that we cannot go past a fear, doubt, or other perceived limitation, we deny the source of our own endlessness!

October 27

The more we help others who refuse to help themselves, the more reasons we give them to remain helpless.

October 28

When we realize that the world around us is powerless to grant our wish for a sense of real permanency, our attention naturally turns toward that uncharted country within us where, as our eyes accustom themselves to the light therein, we catch a glimpse of our eternal home.

That painful sense of urgency, that fiery feeling that comes with anxiously running after something in life thought to be critical to our well being, is one of the ways in which the false self makes what is essentially meaningless into something seen as being highly meaningful.

October 30

The four conditions of happiness are simple: clear eyes, a quiet mind, a sense of beauty, and an open heart. Unhappiness is the dark effect of refusing to cultivate these essential elements for having imagined, by a false light, another kind of contentment that does not exist.

October 31

The gentle strains of great and noble truths pass through the soul in every fleeting moment; and had we but a wish to hear, coupled with the will to be silent for a spell, we would soon detect the sound of our own eternity, sounding out in that silence to which we then would hold so dear.

November 1

The only way to know for sure whether or not life is inherently good is to never again let some pressure-filled fear convince us that without its guidance, something bad will surely befall us. The truth is that once we see there is nothing good about fear, bad things stop happening to us.

November 2

Ultimately, it is the power to serve others that best serves those who wish to know the real riches of life, while those who seek power for themselves serve no one, not even their own best interests.

November 3

Here is how to receive a gift from life greater than can be told: never again give to another person any thought or feeling that you wouldn't want to keep for yourself.

November 4

We do not cheat another when, by cunning or deceit, we seek to gain or otherwise take advantage of him; but we cheat only ourselves of the same moment's power to transform us, to show us that we already possess resources within us so vast that it is we who should be giving to the one from whom we take!

November 5

A painful regret is a needless present pain over an experience now past, where a misstep becomes the seed of a misery mistakenly carried forward, instead of a lesson learned and then dropped.

November 6

Since what others may do to us is not in our power to change, we need only concern ourselves with what we do to ourselves, for this *is* in our power.

November 7

Whenever we ask, "What did I do to deserve this?" we have forgotten that we ask for what we receive with every thought and feeling we embrace and to which we give life. The great axiom with regards to realizing this self-liberating truth is that the plant always reveals the seed.

Work consciously to deliberately drop the names of your pains and you will also learn to let go of all the reasons you have for experiencing them.

November 9

At their outset, right choices are not always free of fear or doubts, but unlike all wrong choices, our right choices never leave us with painful regrets.

Mediocrity is a form of madness, a dream embraced by the masses because it makes just getting by an acceptable—sometimes applauded—social art form. What is excellent requires extra effort. To agree to sleep our way through life is to lose everything, because it rules out the possibility of our soul's awakening.

November 11

Real acts of love never say, "Look at me!"
Real love never flaunts itself, but quietly
gives itself up for the sake of another.

November 12

Whenever we do the very best we can do, give the very most that we have to give, even though we may be far from perfect in that moment, we bring ourselves into the native perfection of that moment. And it is only through learning to endure our own imperfections that we realize Perfection itself is our guide and master.

November 13

Just as we know that we're responsible when a thief steals our car because we left it unattended with the keys in the ignition, so should we realize that we have no one else to blame for how bad we feel whenever we permit negative states to steal into our heart and drive off with it!

November 14

Waiting for a peaceful life to come as a result of what others do is like hoping that you can quench your thirst by watching someone else drink water. Real peace is not an agreement between others; it is a personal act of sacrificing the self that believes others are responsible for the reality it experiences.

November 15

The first cause of unhappiness in our lives is not the negative states that step into our hearts and cause them pain, but that we have forgotten that no darkness exists that is greater than the light that is the life of our True Self.

November 16

Every moment that unfolds in life presents us with an invitation to choose either the path of what will better us—as when we choose conscious kindness over unthinking cruelty—or a path that will make us more bitter—as when we unconsciously embrace a resentment instead of working to release it. To be wise is to choose in favor of the "better path," even though the bitter one often seems easier.

November 17

The pain of knowing that we don't know what to do is only entered into once, while the pain of pretending that we do understand lives on for as long as does our pretense.

November 18

Fear and false self-certainty are secret lov-
ers who have made it a strict rule never to
be seen in the company of each other!

November 19

If only we were one-tenth as sensitive to the kind of thoughts and feelings in which we daily dress our soul as we are compulsively attentive to what clothes we must put on to be pictured well by others, our hearts would be light, our minds bright, and all would be right in our soul.

November 20

The only problem with starring in your own mental movie is that you never want the show to end—so you stop caring about the kind of roles you are given to play!

November 21

When at last you decide you would rather find your own way, you will also find that you have found yourself.

November 22

Spiritual patience is born in us as we grow to realize that our individual lives are forever being revealed in a great clockwork whose tireless and timeless mainspring is Love. Our part in this inexorable movement of life is not to resist what appears untimely in its unfolding but—providing we will remain open, watchful, and honest about what is being revealed—to realize that everything needed for the perfection of our peace does arrive.

November 23

There are two ways to learn about God's life. We can either study past examples of sacrifice and humility, or we can agree to let God use us as living examples of what he wishes us to know about Himself. While the former approach may educate us, only the latter can elevate us into that light and life we wish to know.

November 24

Love delivers life's lessons; it teaches them and is made wise through them. And, in the end, love is the lesson learned.

November 25

What is any display of greatness but the evidence of a love first realized and then suffered to be expressed, revealing timeless invisible perfection in a temporal physical form?

November 26

We affirm the truth—not by professing its powers on sunny days, but in our willingness to walk by its light—even in the midst of those darkest storms where all we can see by this light is just how powerless we are.

November 27

Until we become conscious of how many more times a day we complain about our life than we feel gratitude for the gift of it, we not only miss the taste of life's secret sweetness, but we continue to sow the bitter seeds of our own sorrow.

November 28

All lingering negative states are indigestion
of the mind. They are a kind of chronic resi-
due created by resistance to learning the life
lessons that ride in on the back of events.

November 29

As we awaken to see and receive the inherent good of life that has been hidden in plain sight, so we realize the power to release our fear of unwanted events as surely as perfectly ripened apples fall away from their autumnal tree.

November 30

When God's will becomes our sole wish in life, then whatever happens to us not only fulfills our wish, but we realize it has always been our wish right from the start.

December 1

Before we can know a happiness beyond the reach of conflict or sorrow, we must ourselves be whole; for any happiness apart from self-wholeness is only half a happiness and must, in time, prove itself so.

December 2

In the end, the one who awakens to real life
realizes that it isn't love that he has found,
but that it was love that lead him all along
on his journey home.

Fall / Winter Solstice

December 3

At all costs, be honest with yourself and with those around you, but never believe that the banner of truthfulness you would honor and defend is a license for cruelty or the condemnation of anyone else, including yourself.

December 4

Just as with all tempests in nature, all psychological storms must pass as well; but those who run from their troubles run with them, which is why wherever they go a storm awaits their arrival.

December 5

The work to live in the presence of God costs us nothing except to see that our life, spent in selfish pursuits, costs us everything.

December 6

The only thing "special" about trying to appear unique in the eyes of others is the special kind of suffering that must be endured whenever we pretend to be what we are not.

Fall / Winter Solstice

December 7

Our demands that life be what we want it to be do not make life more desirable; they only hide from us just how undesirable it is to be who we are in that moment.

When we are awakened at night from a nightmare, we realize with a start that we had been sleeping; but when a dark state overcomes us in the daylight hours, we believe we are awake, never suspecting that our bad dream unfolds as it does because we remain asleep within ourselves.

December 9

The conviction we need to make real changes in ourselves comes with this revelation: what we really need isn't another new idea about who we should be, but the grace-granted courage to discontinue being who we have been.

December 10

It seldom occurs to us that whatever we persist with in our lives works to perfect the same, so that by allowing persistent negative thoughts and feelings to have their way with us, we unknowingly perfect self-punishment!

December 11

True strength of character is not just calculated by how well we manage to carry some sizable load under challenging conditions, but is perhaps better measured by our ability to remain kind and light-spirited, even when we're sure that we can't bear the weight of one more ounce of life.

December 12

In time, life makes momentary rulers of us all; but only if we learn to rule ourselves do we lose nothing when kingdoms fade away, as they must!

December 13

Feeling sorry for yourself is like slipping off a boat at sea and, just as you're falling into the water, grabbing the anchor to take with you so as to have something you can cling to in your time of trouble.

December 14

To know that every moment (regardless of how it comes wrapped) is a gift greater than you can give yourself, is to be well on your way to a life without fear.

December 15

We are never punished by life itself, but only by our life choices. This timeless truth helps to explain how the wise can dwell in the exact same world as do the willfully ignorant, but instead of seeing it as a dark, empty, and often painful place, find it to be full of light and rich with promise.

December 16

When we seek this world, we win its gifts that are fashioned in time; but when we seek the celestial, we find ourselves—and discover that living within us is that which made the stars.

December 17

It isn't hard, at times, to love others for what they are. Such relationships are on easy terms, and we receive what we give in a fair measure. But to love others for what they may yet be—to give them the patience and kindness that lets them flower—this is a different task altogether. Loving a person for what he or she may be costs us; and to pay this coin we must, ourselves, run in debt to who it is that we hope to be, an act that requires our payment in every moment and with all those we meet.

December 18

In truth, we are never more lost to ourselves, or to the hope of realizing our own unlimited potential, than when we give ourselves over to the fear of what may become of our lives, for whoever takes fear as a guide follows not just the blind, but is further deceived into believing that its blinding force is the same as some new and higher power of perception!

December 19

Whatever burden we help another person shoulder in life, assuming we see effort being made, strengthens everyone involved by proving that the strength of any weakness is only the degree to which it is feared.

December 20

When the love of God is your guide, you never step into a moment that isn't what you've always been waiting for.

December 21

(Winter Solstice in the Northern Hemisphere)

The real reason why life tests us as it does—trial by trial—is so the strength we are yet to know can be forged within us, as it is with steel—slowly, blow by blow.

December 22

If anxious thoughts and feelings had any power to help us reach some place in life where, finally, we'd be released from the pain of always feeling rushed, don't you think we'd have reached there by now?

December 23

To realize the great liberating truth that we never walk through this life alone, we must spend more time by ourselves!

Before we can know a happiness beyond the reach of conflict or sorrow, we must be whole; for any happiness apart from self-wholeness is only half a happiness and must, in time, prove itself so.

December 25

When we know that life—bare as it may be at times—is the most precious gift of all, then ours is a peace beyond profit and immune to loss.

December 26

We know life by its *movement*—by its parade of passing things, and by our thoughts about them that lend us a ceaseless sensation of ourselves. But to know our True Self, to dwell in its timeless sanctuary through which all the forms of life come and go—then we must know *stillness*.

December 27

Our present mind looks at the universe through what amounts to a pin-prick in a piece of paper and declares, by that minuscule light meeting the eye, that it has seen all there is to see!

December 28

Never speak out of anger,
Never act out of fear,
Never choose from impatience,
But wait . . . and peace will appear.

Fall / Winter Solstice

December 29

We cannot hope to enter into that life larger than our own as long as we continue to look at our own life through a set of limited ideas that preclude that possibility.

December 30

What *really* binds us to any dark mental or emotional world in which we find ourselves suffering is our unquestioned belief that these painful places are the only possibilities that exist for us in that moment. Breaking free from any punishing belief begins with seeing one great truth: were it not for this false conclusion about our unwanted condition, then our sense of being held a captive in these lower worlds would be seen for what it is: *an illusion*.

393

December 31

Real Life is change itself, a ceaseless flow of creative forces expressed in ever-new forms. So, our inability to make a fresh start isn't because life refuses us what we need to succeed. The problem is this: before we can hope to make a real new beginning in life, we must deliberately release our old claims upon it; for it is only in letting go of whatever binds us to our past that we are free to realize the promise of who we may yet be.

Not the End, but the Beginning … Again!

About the Author

Best-selling "Letting Go" author Guy Finley's encouraging and accessible ideas cut straight to the heart of our most important personal and social issues—relationships, success, addiction, stress, peace, happiness, freedom—and lead the way to a higher life. Barnes and Noble says: *"Guy Finley has helped millions live fuller, more peaceable lives."*

Finley is the acclaimed author of *The Secret of Letting Go* and more than 35 other books and audio programs on the subject of self-realization, several of which have become international best sellers. In addition, he has presented over 4,000 unique self-realization seminars to thousands of students throughout North America and Europe over the past 25 years. His popular Key Lesson Newsletter emails are read by 400,000 subscribers in 142 countries each week.

His popular works, published in 16 languages, are widely endorsed by doctors, professionals, and religious leaders of all denominations. Some of his best-loved titles include: *The Secret of Letting Go*, *Design Your Destiny*, *The Lost Secrets of Prayer*, *Apprentice of the Heart*, *Let Go and Live in the Now*, *The Meditative Life*, and *Secrets of Being Unstoppable*.

Finley has been a guest on hundreds of television and radio shows, including national appearances on ABC, NBC, CBS, CNN, and NPR. He is currently syndicated on eight international radio networks, including Healthylife Radio Network, Achieve Radio Network, WorldTalkRadio Network, and Contact Talk Radio.

In addition to his writing and appearance schedule, Finley is the founding director of the Life of Learning Foundation, the renowned non-profit center for self-study located in Merlin, Oregon.

Life of Learning Foundation

Life of Learning is a nonprofit organization founded by author Guy Finley in 1992. Its foremost purpose is to help individuals realize their true relationship with life through higher self-studies. The foundation is operated and run solely by volunteers. Everyone is welcome.

Guy Finley speaks four times each week at the foundation to the men and women who gather there to learn more about self-realization. Everyone is invited to share in the powerful transformational atmosphere that permeates each insight-filled talk. Each meeting awakens new energies, deepens intuitive powers, heals past hurts, and delivers welcome relief.

Life of Learning rests in the heart of southern Oregon's most beautiful country, upon fourteen acres of old-growth sugar pine. Visitors enjoy the beautiful flower gardens, organic foods, and walking trails with special places for meditation along the way. Twice a year, the foundation hosts special retreats for visitors during the third weeks of December and June. The June "Talks in the Pines" event is an annual favorite.

Whether you enjoy wild rivers, scenic lakes, old-growth forests, mountain hiking, or strolling along the rugged Pacific Coast, when you visit Life of Learning you're only minutes away from nature at its best. Life of Learning is located in the community of Merlin, Oregon, near the city of Grants Pass.

To learn more about the work of Guy Finley and Life of Learning Foundation, visit www.guyfinley.org for a wealth of free helpful information, free audio and video downloads, and to request your free starter kit.

FREE CD or DVD

A Special Gift for You

3 Keys to Complete Self-Command
A new breakthrough CD or DVD
from best-selling author Guy Finley

A special gift for buyers of *365 Days to Let Go*
Includes FREE shipping*

Conscious Self-Command is your natural right! With it, all things work in your favor; without it, freedom is impossible.

In this powerful CD or DVD, *3 Keys to Complete Self-Command*, you will discover how to:

- Enter into any challenging situation with supreme confidence
- End the painful stress of comparing yourself to others
- Dismiss any negative thought or emotion
- Face uncertainty without fear of any kind

- Take conscious command of unkind and difficult people
- Use every condition to increase higher self-understanding
- Enrich all of your relationships at home and where you work
- Rise above any self-defeating behavior

Everything you need to know about the source of true self-liberation is available now. Don't miss out! Get your FREE copy of *3 Keys to Complete Self-Command* by author Guy Finley today.

**Visit www.guyfinley.org/365dvd
or call (541) 476-1200
to request your FREE CD or DVD today!**

**Free shipping offer valid for addresses in the U.S. and Canada only.
Please see website for further information and restrictions.*